I Wish I Were Fiction

By

Ruby Moon Churchill

For my family who believe in me always

For the teachers and mentors who gave me the tools

to pursue this particular enjoyment.

Dear Reader,

This book is filled with poems about mental health, love, friendship and so much more. A way to delve into deeper emotions and feelings without needing verbally to express it. Read it any way you like, start to finish, finish to start, pick a number and go with it, whatever floats your boat. But read them carefully, perhaps you'll find something in them that resonates with you. Before you begin, a quick trigger warning, the following contains topics and mentions of mental health problems, intrusive thoughts, eating disorders, abandonment, and death. If any of these things could trigger you while reading, please skip them or put the book down. These poems are not intended to harm anyone in any way, and I ask that you take care of yourself while reading. Poetry and reading are such escapes for me in the best way, and I hope that others may find that in my writing. It has been a wonderful experience writing this and I can't wait for you to read and hopefully enjoy. Now enough waffling on, here begins your poetry journey and I wish you luck on your way.

Words of Wisdom and Love, Ruby Moon. X

1

If you loved me like I loved you,
Would I finally be satisfied?

Or would the longing only transfer
Into something else?

Could I find peace knowing I had your heart?
Or would I constantly long to see you more?

Is it possible that I'd be okay if I could call you mine?

If you loved me like I loved you,
Would my wounds scar or continue to bleed?

I would say the numbness hurts,

But it cannot.

It's numb.

I can't describe to you what it is to feel something,

Nor can I recognise what it is I'm feeling.

I tried to get on a plane in my mind.

It refused to leave the ground.

As hard as I tried to fly my feelings away,

They still refuse to leave me.

I know they are still there,

Hiding.

They come out to greet me sometimes

But oftentimes they cannot control themselves

And I must banish them again.

I float through my days, only existing in the second,

Right now.

I survive and interact as if I were designed to.

But I think I cannot truly be numb,

For I feel it all throughout me.

And it is the worst non feeling of them all.

3

I want to be loved.

Oh God I want to be loved.

And I want to love.

I have so much love to give,

If I could only give it to someone.

I want to give my heart to another

And have them return the exchange.

I want to call someone mine

and have them call me theirs.

So I implore the universe to please,

Find me someone

And give them to me,

For I don't wish to be lonely anymore.

I want to be loved.

You're always so close,

But as soon as I start to reach towards you,

You're a million miles away.

You're oblivious,

You exist in peaceful bliss.

I can hear your voice in the rain,

Hear your laugh in the thunder.

The world becomes you for you are my world.

The future is vast, but I think you are there.

I think I'll find you in rivers, clouds and trees.

When you are not near,

You'll be in the air.

My mind is twisted and turned,

But ahead of all the darkness,

You create such a light

That the sun itself is jealous.

Of all the sounds,

Your voice is the utmost of pulchritude.

You humble mountains and oceans,

Even the stars choose you as their own.

Divinity.

I can feel now what that is.

You make it possible for me.

5

Soft snowfall
Almost whiter than the keys I tap,
Twinkling in the moon's cold glow.
The cold welcome,
And turned warm by the joy I feel.

The music takes hold of my mind,
A firm but comforting grip.
Losing myself in the rhythm,
My surroundings melt away;
Leaving me alone with nothing but
My thoughts,
And the notes.

My story started as a slow burn drama,

A few twists and turns,

A couple stops and starts.

Page after page

It went on and on,

Dragging here and there,

Taking a dip,

Starting up again.

I often felt it was not my own story,

I'd be a better side character

For I am seldom seeking your attention.

Background characters came and went,

Occasionally interacting,

Oftentimes only making cameos.

Then came along a character

whom I did not see in my story.

The story took a turn,

Chapters taking on a new subplot.

The stop signs blocked off the path

And forced a new route.

I plunged a hole in the Earth,

Made a new road and formed a tunnel

Through all the plot gaps.

A twist has never caught me off guard,

There's always been something to warn.

But not this time,

Not this twist...

And what a twist you were.

The way in which we view the world

Relies solely on what we perceive to be beautiful.

The difference between good and bad,

Light and dark.

One's soul determines how we associate the things we see.

Someone sees the ocean and feels calm and serene.

Someone sees the ocean and begins to panic.

Someone passes a stranger in the street,

Another gets lost in their eyes for an hour.

We are predisposed to love and hate,

But what if that could change?

What if breaking down walls as high as mountains

Could widen the horizon

And force someone to see more than they did before,

See the truth perhaps?

For viewing the world as beautiful

Is a skill not many have learned.

Instead of favouring light over darkness,

Have them co-exist.

Choose to see things not how you're told,

But as they are,

Truly.

My soul says the world looks more wonderful

Through your eyes,

So today, as my beautiful thing,

I choose you.

8

I came across a tree

Standing alone in a field.

Tall and broad

But decorated with no leaves.

It was not used as a rest stop for many creatures,

The crows being the most frequent visitors.

Even though it could be regarded

As a desolate or useless tree,

It gives me a sense of comfort,

Every time I drive past that field.

To know that it'll be there,

Alone but still standing strong.

Alone, but mighty.

If you were asked to describe happiness,

What would you say?

To jumpstart your imagination, I will give you my answer.

Happiness looks like a book and a blanket,

A candle and rain.

Walks in a warm summer breeze,

A light-coloured dress and a shady willow tree.

A warm, scented bath, evenings by the fire,

Music and baking, the perfect attire.

Happiness is coloured like rainbows,

It tastes so sweet.

It smells like flowers and feels so safe.

I wish to cling to it, though sometimes it must leave me.

It's on my mind all the time,

Wishing I could feel its warmth.

It does not seem to want me much,

Though I feel it with me always;

Just too far to touch.

Happiness feels like everything and anything,

And if I could,

I'd wrap it all up, a bundle of joy.

I would take every molecule of goodness and love,

Put them together and give them a name.

Your name.

For you are the very embodiment of my happiness.

You are everything I've just described and more.

So if you were to ask me to describe the word happiness,

I would simply give them,

Your Name.

If you were asked to describe pain,

What would you say?

Use your imagination, I'll give you my answer to help you think.

Pain is the clouds that follow me around.

Pain is cold too heavy to escape.

Pain is the smell of smoke;

you know that fire is near but you cannot find it.

Pain is dark and infinite,

The abyss stretches further and further until nothing more is visible.

No light, no colour.

It seems to want me more than ever,

It's the only one that does.

I welcome it with open arms and listen to its woes.

It's always been there,

The only constant I now seem to know.

Pain is hidden in anything and everything,

So close and so far.

If I could, I would gather it all,

Every spec of darkness and despair,

And I would name it.

With Your Name.

For Noble Musicians will no longer play,

And your light falls dim,

Defeated by heartbreak and forgotten promises.

So ask for a description of pain;

I'll give them,

Your Name.

If I had to miss you like this again,

I think I'd crumble.

If I had to hurt like this again,

I would break.

It's a miracle to me how one person

Can cause my very existence

To balance on a knife edge,

Without slipping.

But you're not beside me anymore.

And I can feel the sharp edge getting closer.

I'll never be rid of you.

Your face in my memories,

Your voice in my ear.

My only comfort stems from staring at the stars and the moon,

Knowing,

That somewhere,

You're staring at them too.

I'm disconnected from myself.

I've felt it before but this time it is different.

I know I can make it feel more whole,

But my mind keeps taking the opinions of others as law.

I hear it everyday,

And I know it is right, but it feels so binding.

I am trying to learn to unravel my ways,

Teach myself that I'm allowed to want and need to change.

But each time I hear it

It gets that little bit worse.

I will still hear it, but I know those closest will hear me instead.

I needn't force myself into the shell of a person the world wishes me to be.

I am allowed to be me.

Be free.

I'll listen to what my souls says I need.

I hope to the Gods that I will be heard.

13

The best kind of love is not romantic.
The absolute best kind of love can be described in many or little words,
Such as:

Knowing you would die for each other.

Never wanting anything more than to look at their face and be in their company for always.

Calling them only to pretend you're not there, an inside joke only you'll understand.

Having a language you created that sounds like nonsense to the rest of us.

Waking up each and every day knowing that out there is a person who would do anything for you.

Telling anyone you'd absolutely sell them for a piece of cake, knowing in your heart you wouldn't
give them up for the world.

The best kind of love I've seen, is the love between two people,
destined to live separate lives, while always finding their way back to each other, sharing one heart.

As for the little word description, these people can simply be called,

Platonic Soulmates.

14

Our love is not poetry and it never will be.

We will not see ourselves in the stars,
Nor will we carve our initials in tree bark.

We will never be the souls intertwined by the universe,
destined to find each other and conquer all evil with love.

We will be the hearts who worked, were broken and mended.
We see the journey we've been on
and will continue down that path,

Hand in hand,
Combating obstacles,
Always overcoming.

Because you amplify my heart like nothing has before.
With you I am whole.

15

Sleep has never been my friend.

Ever since I was a child, the monsters under the bed would call out,
and make my dreams seem a treacherous place.

Now my room is free of shadows,
The monsters however still loom.
But instead of crawling from under the bed,
The monsters now live in my head.

So though sleep can be an escape,
It seems the door is locked.
I tug and tug, this way and that,
Never getting free.

I ask you, time and time again,
Will you ever let me be?

16

I think comfort is one of my favourite feelings.
It's just such a nice, calming sensation.

Complete calm.
To find an environment that creates such a calm in you is one of the best experiences.

Whether this be a place, a movie, a person even.
Having a person be your source of comfort is such a unique, wonderful thing.

This is why comfort is so important,
Relief from stress,
Being able to unwind and relax.
Without needing to worry,
Knowing everything is under control and nothing needs to be done.

I think it will always be my favourite feeling.
I hope to feel it again soon.

I look at you, and all that comes to mind is
Wow.
Look at this divine creation stood before me.

Do you not see the incredible
Beauty
I am surrounded with?

I am sure you are made from the highest
Power.
Perfection was named after you.

Not only are you the most breath-taking
Angel
I have ever had the honour of knowing,

But you have a beauty that carries inwards,
Caring
as deeply as you do.

You are quite simply the most beautiful person I have ever in my life gazed upon or spoken to.

And you needn't work to keep this up,
You simply being you,
Will always be enough for me.

18

Yours is the only hand I ever want to hold.

Palm to palm, I've never felt more at home.

Your touch is all the promises in the world and I swear to never let go.
Not until my hands are scarred and burning,
Not until the earth swallows me whole.

I will love you until the day the sun sets upon this planet with intent to destroy.
I think perhaps even after that.

For your love is all I have ever needed, and all I could ever want.
Even if you leave me someday, this love will always find me.
It shall rival shadow, vanquish enemies.

Yours is the only hand I ever want to hold,
Please take mine in return.

19

I'm afraid of my body.
I'm afraid of what it is.
I know and can recognise what a wonderful creation it is,
But it scares me.

I can't stand in pictures.
It's a constant thought in the back of my head,
How to hide, change and alter myself to fit society's standards which have infected my mind.

I hate that I don't look like them.
I wish I could change it.
But I can't.
I'll have to learn to live with myself,
Even if I'm miserable the rest of my life,
Always worrying,
Always wondering.

If I were beautiful,
Would they like me more?

If I could be beautiful,
Could I finally look in the mirror?

20

I want to be seen by someone.
I want to be noticed.
Not in the spotlight sense of noticed,
I want someone to *see* me.

I want them to see me, like me, love me even.
Is that so much to ask for?

Is my life planned out on a timeline?
Waiting for the right moment?
Or am I so flawed that no one should ever take interest in me?

I just want to be seen and loved for me.
I don't want to feel the shame I keep feeling when I make any singular move.

It's like I'm being taunted,
not knowing what will happen next,
if I'll mess up and fall as I always do,
or whether this time,
I might finally be caught.

Dear me, 8 years ago.

You're running.
I know you are,
I feel it too.
You're running away from all the things you don't understand,
All the things inside your head that are scaring you.
I know it's dark,
I'm ever so sorry you had to feel it.
I couldn't protect you then,
But I will now.
You'll never have to feel it again.
I'll take it away.
Give it to me and I'll make it go away.
You deserve so much more.
You deserve the happiness you didn't think you needed.

You were too young to bear all the pain and suffering you sat through.
You handled it so well,
But you mustn't think it your responsibility to feel it all inside,
In silence.
There's so much I know now that I wish you could know.
I won't tell you it'll be ok,
I know you won't believe me.
But I can promise you,
I am here to protect you now.

I miss you, I'm so sorry, you can breathe now.

22

Give me a book any day of the week.

Let me dive into the pages and live in the shoes of these characters
so I don't have to be here.

I want to escape to worlds of dragons and magic,
Places where the heroes are complicated and the villains aren't all they seem.

It's so much easier to sympathise
with fictional people than to involve myself in real people drama.

Wouldn't it be wonderful if I could walk straight into the chapters
and know that I get a guaranteed ending,
whether happy or sad?

So give me a book any day of the week,
You might just see me disappear.

I am alone a lot.

I like being alone.

Sure I feel lonely sometimes,

Maybe my thoughts are a little louder by myself,

But I like being alone.

My heart might ache a little more alone,

Perhaps my mind wonders to things I don't want without distraction,

But I don't need company.

I. Like. Being. Alone.

I know I do.

I need to be alone.

I am safer by myself.

24

My mirror is cracked.

In a way, it makes my reflection more true.

My mirror sees what others don't.

I've never seen so many cracks on a person.

It's a wonder they don't break.

At least you can't see inside,

See all of my mistakes.

I could just replace it so it's no longer broken,

But it reflects a piece of me that doesn't always show.

So I think I'll hold onto it, just a little while longer,

Just in case I need to remember.

Just in case I need to remember, me.

I am grieving.

I'm going through all the stages at once.

I am grieving, but I don't know what for.

I miss those I've lost but this pain is fresh, new.

I think perhaps when I think too deeply,

I am grieving the little girl with my name,

The little girl no bigger than a wagon wheel,

With a big smile on her face and not a worry in the world.

I think I grieve for her.

I think I'm missing the life that was taken from her.

The joy and the hope that filled her future she didn't think about too often,

Replaced with darkness and despair,

Not even sure the future's there anymore.

I feel the need to apologise to her.

Tell her I'm sorry for all her pain and hurting.

She doesn't deserve it.

She did nothing wrong.

I wish I could tell her it'll be alright,

That we'll make it through,

But the truth is,

I can't tell her because I don't believe it's true.

She was beautiful and pure.

Innocent and carefree.

The world gave her scars and told her to be cautious,

So I can't be like her anymore.

I try to protect her.

I couldn't keep her safe before,

When I *was* her,

But now she'll never hurt again.

I will take all the darkness and pain.

Her mind was a beautiful place,

Colourful and creative.

Clouds have overshadowed that now.

She could've been a wondrous creature,

But she couldn't be saved.

She died with you,

And out of the ash and rubble I was created.

I will keep her safe now.

Little one, I'm so sorry you had to see the world as it truly is.

It shouldn't have harmed you as it did.

I think I also have grief for my future.

Or at least, the future I wish to have.

I think constantly of everything I wish to have

And keep on wishing every day to take me somewhere I can be

In this idealistic future of mine

With all the things I wish to have or be.

I wish for a house, safety, warmth, comfort.

I wish for family, sacred, precious, mine.

Dancing under moonlight,

Held onto by tiny fingers.

Decorating a living room,

First laughs, first words, first steps.

I wish for this and so much more.

It's a new, specific type of hurt that this causes.

It's a happy, almost memory,

Of a time not yet occurred.

I don't know if it will ever occur.

But I think my fleeting hope that comes every so often

Is focused on the image of my utopia,

With everything I could have hoped to accomplish in a lifetime.

Anemoia is the feeling of missing a time you've never known,

I believe my life to be a perfect example of this concept,

And my heart hurts so much because of it.

Dear Sadness,

You bind me.

How dare you.

How could you take away the life that was mine?

Dear Sadness,

I hate you.

I hate you more than anything for everything you've done to me.

Dear Sadness,

Your hand on my shoulder isn't welcome.

I would cut it from your arm to be rid of at least a small part of you.

Dear Sadness,

Why?

Dear Sadness,

I can't breathe.

Dear Sadness,

Let me go.

Please.

My angels in the sky,

You look wonderful in the clouds.

Like you were made to roam the skies and be the stars.

Though some selfish part of me wishes you'd never left me.

I wish you'd never said goodbye.

You didn't see me to 2.

You didn't see me to 10.

You left me at 12.

You couldn't watch me grow.

You weren't here for me when I needed you.

But I can't be angry.

You didn't choose to leave me.

You had to go.

I wonder if you'd like me now,

Be proud of what I've done.

I had to learn to live without you.

Life doesn't look so good without you here.

I miss you,

And I will miss you for the rest of my life.

I will miss you until the very second I can be with you again.

I want a fairy tale.

But then again I don't.

They often entail some daring act of bravery,

Which I dare say I don't have.

What I want is the magic,

The happy ever after.

I've always wanted one of those.

I've been told it doesn't exist,

That true love is simply fiction.

I think that's why I find it in stories,

Pieces of me scattered in the pages.

Because if I look at the words for long enough,

I start to hear their voices.

If I believe hard enough,

Perhaps I'll become one of them,

With my own fairy tale,

With all the magic and wonder one could ever dream of.

I'm still shaking.

The terror is gone but something still lingers.

It's dark, but I can't bring myself to switch on the lamp.

I don't think I can move from this spot.

I won't move ever again.

Perhaps I died in that moment,

Perhaps this is the purgatory I deserve.

No, I can hear voices from downstairs.

I am still alive.

I am still alive.

Though how can that be?

I thought I'd surely died in there.

In that darkness.

It swallowed me.

I felt it.

It surrounded me and I couldn't escape.

I don't remember entirely what happened.

I only felt the fear.

How am I breathing when a moment ago I had no air in my lungs?

My heart has stopped I'm sure of it.

I'm waiting for the floor to open up beneath me.

Falling through the Earth would be better than this torment.

I'm still shaking.

Everything hurts yet I can feel,

Nothing.

I like hearing someone else take my thoughts and put them to music.

It's easier to relate to someone else's voice than it is to use my own.

I could make whole stories,

Have full conversations,

Using the songs I listen to everyday.

They will tell you my story.

Learn about me through my music.

It's a lifeline I didn't know I desperately needed.

The right voice singing the right words at the right time.

It's an entire universe condensed into a few minutes.

Over and over again I will listen,

If only to immerse myself in someone else's mind.

Just for a little while.

It's a curious thought that you have a mind of your own.

That you don't just live in my world,

I live in yours.

You live in your own mind,

with thoughts and feelings I know nothing of.

It's a curious thought and I'm not sure I like it.

I will never know what you truly think of me.

I can ask but I'll never be sure you tell me the truth.

I don't like it.

I am seen differently by everyone around me.

Countless people have glanced me walking by,

A perfect stranger.

I don't like it.

I live around other people and I don't like it.

I will never trust you again.
Never again.
You will never crawl back into my veins to be my blood and keep me breathing.
You will never infect my mind,
Condition me to love you,
Not like you did the first time.
I have learned.
I may learn slowly with you
But at least
I learn.

I have known enough pain from you
To know the warning signs.
I recognise the way your voice changes
When you're trying to manipulate.
You tend to be good at that.
But I won't let you do it.

Not
Ever
Again.

33

Tomorrow I will wake in my bed,
Wishing to go back to sleep.

Tomorrow I will brush my teeth with mint toothpaste,
Turn on the tv and breakfast on whatever I can find.

Tomorrow I will wish I didn't have to go out,
I'll want to stay home and do boring things.

But I will be grateful for all these things,
I will love the fact that I get to be sad and bored,
I may not like my life,
I may wish for everything to change a lot of the time,

But you didn't get a tomorrow,
So I will live my tomorrows for you,
Every one for you.

Please come with me.

I know you're scared,

You don't want to leave your Earth friends.

It's important I deliver you to your destination.

I am not what you wanted.

I know this.

I am no angel,

I am only dark and lonely.

I promise my hood is to protect me from the sun,

I promise this scythe is only for my garden.

I am merely a guide,

You needn't be afraid.

Please don't fear me,

I hate being scary.

I am so lonely,

All of the time.

And I see her.

Shining as she should,

Beloved creator,

Sacred keeper.

She cannot be mine.

We cannot even brush hands.

You will be safe where you're going,

Just follow me,

We won't be travelling long.

Good luck on your adventures,

Your friends and family will grieve,

But they will be alright.

Enjoy your happy eternity,

I will suffer mine,

Always feared,

Always alone.

I called you a friend,

Loved you at one point.

That wasn't enough for you, was it?

You had to go and **ruin** it.

We were good.

You were **deceiving**.

Sly.

Conniving.

Of all the people it had to be you.

I denied it for as long as I could.

No more.

You will **feel** what I felt.

I will make you **regret** every word you said.

You obviously didn't realise

the knife you stuck in my back was double bladed.

We can look up and see their face;

They're reading again.

Everyone take their places,

This will be the best re-telling they've ever had.

Our world may only be a story to them,

Fiction,

But to see the smile on their face at a favourite line,

Getting into arguments about who made them laugh the most,

Crying with them as we watch our friends fall again.

This is the magic we love to create.

It is wonderful to share in our tale so many times with them.

They know how it will end,

But they don't mind.

Only, when they reach the last page,

Last line,

Last word,

I find I'm not ready to say goodbye,

Don't shut it now,

I don't want to go…

I don't try to fix our conversations anymore.

It's easier to give up than to try to return to my point.

You never gave me the communication I needed.

So I respond with "oh".

Oh.

Okay then.

On the outside,

"oh" is okay, a casual end and acknowledgement.

In my heart,

"Oh" is really,

Ow, you just tore out *another* piece of me.

You really don't care, do you?

I'm sorry I couldn't be enough for you,

So go, set yourself free from me if it's so hard for you.

Just stop hurting me like this.

A way's away from anywhere she lives alone in an abandoned house.

It's cold.

She doesn't mind.

A way's away from anyone she stays awake until dawn.

She's lonely.

She doesn't mind.

A way's away from internet she reads until she can't see anymore.

She's isolated.

She doesn't mind.

She lives alone in an abandoned house in the cold with no one and nothing to keep her company.

Everyone she once knew is gone, in one way or another, they left her.

She's alone.

But she doesn't mind.

I can't stand the fact that you hate me.

I can't stand the fact that I love you.

What did I do to make you care so little about me?

Is it that you shall never love?

Or am I just too unlovable for you to even try?

I've had to fight for love my entire life,

This time I just wanted it to be easy.

I suppose I'm just too damaged, too fragile.

You can't even look at me.

I look at you and see the sun,

You light up my life but you burn me too often.

40

My villain Queen would bring the world to its knees for me and only me,
But I wonder if it is for what I mean it to be.

Could this stay a gesture of love and devotion,
Instead of turning to a parting gift?

For often we see at the end of a story,
Villains don't receive a happy ever after,
The hero gets that.
Of course they do.

But for once I want my story to end happily,
For once I want to see the hero feel an ounce of the pain they don't think we go through.

The hero tried to save the world by putting me in the way.
My villain tried to burn the world without a single flame touching me.

Now I will burn the rest in her honour.

41

Time is a thief.

It will steal you away from me.

It will take everything I love.

And I can't stop it.

Life may seem a very long time,

But really it is far too short.

I could try to freeze the picture of us,

Keep you close and never out of sight,

But in the end,

Time will take you from me.

It is a race I cannot win.

Late night talks with you are my favourite.

When I can lie with you entwined in my arms, barely awake enough to understand me.
You won't remember this in the morning.

But this is my favourite time,
where I can tell you how much you mean to me in whispers and loving looks in the dark.
You can't see me, but I feel you staring.

My love you are the world to me.
I could not ask for anything more.

My darling you are the moon's most difficult adversary,
and somehow,
you're mine.

I am in awe of you everyday.

You are the most ethereal creation I have ever beheld
and my god I would gaze on you every second if I could.

I love you.
More than anything.

Late nights like this,
mornings when I wake up with your hand in mine,
your eyes looking through to the deepest parts of me.

You are everything I live for,
I only wish you weren't just in my head.

43

There was a mistake in the scheduling I'm sure.
Someone pressed a wrong button somewhere.

I should not be here.
Not in this time.

Someone build a Time Machine,
Take me to when I belong.

It is not fair that I'm forced to live in a time I do not know.

I know 200 years ago,
It's a problematic time,
But at least we were working against it.

I expected the present to be joyful and worth our efforts.
But all I found was new ways to waste our work.
How many people had to suffer for you to throw away our progress?

So I want to go back.
To my time and our fight.
At least then we had hope of change.

So ready my Time Machine,
For surely the 21st Century was not for me.

44

You gave me flowers as a sign of affection.
You said they reminded you of me,
Of the walks we took in the garden,
You knew how I loved the white roses.

I'm more of an Orchid person now.

It felt as though, as the days went by,
Your love for me was tethered to those roses.
They were beautiful and lovely,
As you seemed to me.

Then they began to wilt and wither away,
Looking less like the flowers I had once loved.

Every day I'd look at them on the sill of the window,
I'd tended to them just as I should,
Nurtured them, protected them, kept them well.
But still they wither and there is nothing I could have done.

The last petal fell today.
Your name is gone from my phone and I'm sat here,
trying to forgive.

I don't love white roses anymore.
I can smile at the Orchids on the sill.

Your face doesn't register with me anymore.

It is changed.

The warm smile and kind eyes I knew don't exist now.

I don't know if it was a guise,
Or whether you didn't mean to hurt me,
Only you were lost in yourself.

I think a lot of people would tell me not to make excuses for you.
But the simple truth is that I would still do anything for you.
I would stand in the way of a train if it meant saving you.

You probably could've stopped if you tried.
If you wanted to, you wouldn't have betrayed me.
It probably wasn't your fault.
You probably didn't mean to.

But in the back of my head there's a voice screaming at me to see.

You did hurt me.
You meant to.

It is better to stop loving you and heal,
Than to love you and break.

46

I love you are three words I will never truly believe.
I want to believe them,
Each time you say it to me I want to know in my heart that you mean it.
I want to hear you say it,
Even if my mind makes me doubt it,
I want to hear you say I love you.

I love you.
No you don't.

I love you.
You shouldn't.

I love you.
I don't believe you.

I love you.
I love you too.

The words I will always say,
But never truly believe.

My mind is my own worst enemy.
It's so easy to get in my own head and think myself into a panic.

Most often it starts with
"What if?"
Or "What's the point?"
What is worth living for and far off events in the future that I know I can't stop.

If you asked me what my worst fear is,
I'd probably tell you spiders or the unknown.
But in truth it is the previously mentioned starting points for panic attacks that scare me most of all.

I know I cannot change nor prevent the future
as much as I wish I could,
I will lose everyone I look at and I can't do anything to change that.

I am not in control of my thinking and I think I hate this most.
I cannot escape the images and audios my mind creates as methods of torture for itself.
That's just it,
my mind is a self destructive organ
that doesn't know what the hell it wants,
needs or can't handle.

You wonder why I'm sad while I have nothing to be sad about,
But if you were in my head I guarantee you'd never ask that again.

I live with myself 24/7 and I wish for just a moment I could have a break.

But I cannot.

So once again, sat in dark or daylight,
My thoughts will wander to Why.

The first time I saw you,

it felt like a cool breeze on a hot day,

The perfect end to a movie,

Along with every good thing in the world.

I did not choose to be this way,

It took a long time to accept the fact that I cannot change who I am.

But now,

I would not change it for the world.

It comes with its share of hardships,

The ignorance of people comes out in their words.

They do not try to understand nor accept what does not affect them,

They ridicule,

Tease.

But through the hatred of unnecessary prejudice,

I have found a community,

People so drawn to each other it's as if they were family.

So now when I look at you,

Those good feelings are not shrouded in fear and doubt,

Instead I stand on the shoulders of every queer person before me,

They lift me up and help me to embody every authenticity within me.

I have found my people in the small world we created,

Even the most of my fear is quashed

when the warmth of the love and acceptance within this place shines.

Nothing is black and white,

I now see in rainbows.

And I could not have more Pride in us.

I hope the people on this Earth after us;

If they are there,

Do better than us.

Our generation means well,

but we are losing this planet at a rate I fear we cannot contend with.

Living has become one of the hardest things a person can do.

You are the ones who will outlive us.

You are already burdened with our mistakes and failures.

I apologise for this unfair handicap in the race,

But I'm sure you will learn to run just fine.

I wonder will you discover where we made our fatal error?

Will you discover perhaps there was nothing we were to do?

Or will you confirm that we triggered it all?

We were the start of the end.

I am not a hopeful person,

But I have hope enough that you will at least be able to live for a time

on our beautiful planet,

Maybe you won't know the forests and nature,

Perhaps you won't recognise the animals we grew up learning,

But maybe you will learn to appreciate the Earth you live on now,

Instead of missing the one we lost.

It's a sort of quiet, dark contentedness I've grown so used to in my time.

Misery.

It's funny that we should name it such a thing

when the thing itself is merely a concept.

It is a permanently unwanted guest,

Adhered to my mind in the most inconvenient of places.

It allows me to function a lot of the time,

All the while binding me in a contract I have no recollection of signing,

Enacting the fine print I was not permitted to read every so often,

Shutting down all abilities,

Functions

And capabilities.

Misery is the worst employer ever to invade my life.

Unfortunately, I am in no position to break a non-existent contract.

This is now what I know best.

I cannot let it go.

It is a race between me,

My lungs,

And the water.

Who will succeed in their attempt?

Will the water invade my lungs and force the oxygen to fail?

Will my body prevail and bring me above water before the end?

Will I decide to float or sink?

It's oddly comforting down here,

The pressure of the water is hurting my ears

But I hardly notice anymore.

It's blended into the mess of panic exchanged for curious calm.

I could just stop.

Give up on my lungs trying to keep me conscious,

Admire the shine of the blue as the light reflects off the waves,

Who knows what awaits me in the dark of the ocean?

I've lost track of up, down,

I couldn't tell you my name if I tried.

The ocean is one of those pretty things that hold most dangerous power.

It invites you in before it drags you to your inevitable end.

And as I break the surface the air burns my throat,

I can't see,

I'm scared,

The water feels much scarier when I'm surrounded by the air.

You're walking around as if you're transparent.

You've stopped speaking,

Stopped sleeping,

Stopped eating,

I fear you won't last much longer,

It breaks my heart to see you start to slip away like this.

What has the world done to you that I must watch you fall into darkness

Without being able to save you?

I don't think I know you anymore.

You no longer resemble the person I used to love so dearly.

You don't seem to know me either.

You look at me with a blank expression on your face,

Green eyes gone glassy from tears.

I always loved looking at your eyes,

The shade of oak leaves and ferns,

I could walk through a forest just looking into your eyes.

To have you look at me now hurts too much.

The forest has burned it seems,

There is only despair hidden in the depths of the green.

I wish for you to come back to me everyday.

But I know I cannot pull you from this pit of hopelessness.

I will always need you here,

But you're walking around

As if you were a Ghost.

As if you were a Ghost,

I used to say,

Now your transparency is real,

Memories the only form of you left to me.

It is cruel that I still glimpse you in the corner of my eye,

I turn,

You're not there.

I know you're not but you still seem to haunt me.

I understand now the pain you were swallowed by,

But I made you a promise long ago,

I will live for you,

You amazing angel,

I will live my days and the days you couldn't.

You will never be gone from me though I cannot see you anymore.

I will learn to sit through the hurting

And come to know the other side of it.

It was too much for you,

But I will take your strength and mine

And learn to live in limbo.

Denial.

Anger.

Bargaining.

Depression.

Acceptance.

No, grief is not linear. It could look like anything, it could look like this:

Calm. Realisation. Disbelief.

Denial

Repetition, Blame Placing, Control.

Anger

Delaying, Routine, Hatred.

Bargaining

Manic, Dysregulation, Dissociation.

Depression

Numbness, Appreciation, Fondness.

~~Acceptance~~

Content

Peonies thrive in the coldest of winters.

Winterberries enjoy the cold most of all.
Though it's leaves may drop,
The red shines against the snow.

Catmint survives through the harshest conditions.

Mountain Rock Cress doesn't mind the cold or heat.

Moonflowers bloom when illuminated by moonlight.

These flowers can thrive in all kinds of difficulty,
They battle cold and rain
And still they are the prettiest things nature gives.

I am no flower,
But I just might survive this.

56

Half of me met half of you on a train.

Half of me fell in love with half of you.

We were both broken pieces of a whole.
I thought we could fix each other,
Make each other better.

We could've been so good,
But you needed more than what you had.

Half of me fell in love with half of you.
All of you left me,
Broken,
Empty.
In the end, half of me made you whole.

The bravest thing you can do in your life is live.

Instead of just surviving,

Doing enough each day to stay alive,

Live your life,

Do all the things you've dreamed of doing.

Meet people,

Work because you want to,

Not because you have to.

Accomplish things you didn't think possible.

It may feel like you've been here a long time,

But our time is really too short.

It is hard to not know what awaits you in the future,

It is so hard to continue every day,

Without knowing there's a purpose,

Always aware of whether there's a tomorrow.

It is easier to give in to the unsettled feeling of living,

To keep surviving,

Just enough to be a person,

But instead you could *live,*

Have the life you want,

Be your own person.

This is the bravest thing a person can do.

Give yourself permission to live.

Most eyes are burdened with tears.

Most are flooded, clouding the eyes and making them look lost.

Not you.

You seem to embody your tears,

They compliment your eyes,

Almost as if they're made of glass.

Other people have an entire physical reaction to crying,

They will shake, sob, perhaps fall to the floor.

But you,

You express pain in all the elegance one could have,

You stand silent,

Still,

The tears down your face appear almost like gold.

Looking into your eyes while they're swimming in tears,

I could see a whole universe of your pain,

It was beautifully terrible,

It seemed brighter than it should.

Your eyes are my favourite thing in the world to look at,

Even if they are filled with tears.

59

How dare you love me?!

I have shown you all the warning signs,
All the reasons to run
And yet you love me anyway.

Why?

I have told you there is nothing good to come of me,
There is nothing here for you to love and yet somehow you have found a way.

I want to love you back
But I cannot let you ruin yourself by loving me.
I won't let you waste your love on a shadow.

Nor will I let myself get close to you because if I do there's no going back.
If I let myself look at you for longer than a glance,
I won't ever look away.
I'll get attached,
I'll need you,
But I can't let you love me.

I remember running.

I remember fields of daisies.

I remember warm fires on cold nights.

I remember feeling safe.

I remember feeling wanted.

I remember feeling loved.

I remember us.

61

I can hear you crying far away.

I want to run to you,

Calm you,

Comfort you,

Save you in some way.

But I cannot reach you.

I won't get there in time.

I cannot find you,

Your wailing getting fainter and fainter.

I can only sit and listen in shock

As my skeleton starts to crumble

And I remember I cannot get to you.

Your tears can't be stopped by my ghostly hand.

Winter is on my tongue again

And the leaves doused in white crunch beneath my boots.

The familiar comfort of the cold is here again.

Taken away was the heat of the sun,

Replaced with clouds and rain.

A lot would despise this particular change,

But I revel in it,

Taking in every snowflake,

Every gentle breeze.

I am most at home in the cold,

It is much more welcoming,

Easier to embrace than it is to hide from the sun.

On a Saturday morning,

sat in the armchair by the window,

Is where the sunrise hits you best.

It reflects in the hue of your eye

just enough that I could be convinced you are made of stardust.

I tend not to have a wonderful sense of direction,

But somehow,

I always end up back in your eyes.

You captured me with a glance,

And you do not let me go.

And I do not wish you to.

Not ever.

Do not ever let go of me.

Not even when I'm so sceptical of your love I cannot look at you.

Do not let go when you're mad at me for being scared.

Please, just don't ever let go of me.

64

I smile to you to say hello,

A non-verbal greeting.

You smile back at me but it doesn't look right.

You smile with such hidden sadness,

You put away your suffering in the presence of others,

So as to be there for them.

But who is there for you?

Who sits and listens to your thoughts?

Who hears you when no one else will?

Your sad smile will haunt me,

Knowing I can do nothing to brighten it.

However,

I will do what I am able,

By smiling to you each day,

A non-verbal greeting meant for so many unsaid words.

65

I'm so ready to be over you.

I am ready for you to be gone from me,

But my heart insists you stay.

66

You are not yourself.

You are what others have made you.

You are what you think you must be.

But wouldn't it be wonderful

To stop pretending?

To be whatever and whoever *you* like,

Instead of adjusting to the situation around you?

You shouldn't be expected to suppress yourself

For other's comfort.

You are an individual being,

A creation so unique to this world.

Do not hide it,

Learn to live with yourself,

How *you* want to live.

Your inability to stop giving will be your downfall.

It is a wonderful thing to be as generous as you are,
But others will take advantage of this.

You've never taken from others,
Even those who ridicule you
Feel the warmth of your kindness.

This is why I protect you as I do.
Not because you are weak,
You are not weak.

I protect you because your goodness,
Is not what the world is ready for.
Hopefully it will be one day,
But for now,
You are too good for this world.

68

Often,

What is right and what is good

Are not one in the same.

Sometimes the right thing requires you walk the hardest path.

Sometimes what is easy is not what is right.

It is important to distinguish which is which,

As one could be more disastrous than the other.

Both have consequences,

You will lose and gain things either way you go,

But ultimately,

One will do more good than the other.

69

Solitary in the dark,

Sounds of engines trundling overhead.

A squawk,

An echo,

It bounces over every surface.

The whispers through the wind

Carry messages to the trees,

Passing through this dark tunnel,

My favourite of places,

Where I can simply exist in a world of my own making,

With the sounds of secrets and unsaid stories.

A thousand memories have been made down here,

Now it is my turn to bring life into the echo of a dark tunnel.

Lean on me when you need it.

Don't hide from me when I can clearly see your pain.

Use me as a sounding board.

I don't care if you destroy me in the process,

I will put myself back together for you,

Every

Time.

You will need me.

I know you want to be solely independent,

You hate to rely on anyone.

But I will be there.

Every time you call for me,

I will come running.

You can tear me down,

Pretend you hate me,

Curse me for helping you,

Curse yourself for needing it.

I will always be there with you.

I will always have comfort, support, and solace.

I will **not** let you break yourself from the inside out.

I will be there with you.

I will fix you.

Every.

Single.

Time.

71

I keep telling you

I'm tired.

You keep telling me

To sleep.

You

Still

Don't

Understand.

72

Yellow glow reserved only for my eyes and the stars.

So familiar yet so strange.

The most connected I've been to something not human.

The moon,

My friend in the sky.

Accompanying the stars so they aren't alone.

Not often is the moon a whole,

So when it is,

We appreciate it most.

But even in its pieces,

The moon teaches us it's ok to be broken and beautiful.

When I opened the door and found you waiting,

It was the happiest moment I've ever known.

Flowers in your hand,

A loving look on your face.

If only I had known it was a lie.

Taken from another's vase,

You gave me tainted flowers.

Your 'loving' look stolen from someone else's eyes.

Every promise.

Every compliment.

Every happy moment.

Gone.

You took them from me.

You took up so much space in my heart.

Every inch of that is now rotted,

Dead.

As are you to me.

Did you leave me?

Did you care?

Do I miss you?

Why do I need you so much?

Why are you the best and worst thing I know?

Did you even like me?

Did I make any difference to you?

Did you want me?

At all?

Why am I like this?

Why did you call me?

Why did I cry?

After you leave me, will you forget?

Was I not enough?

Were you simply cruel?

Why do I *still* want you?

Why can't I let go?

Can you leave my head?

Can I feel this?

Can you?

Will it stop?

Eventually?

75

I couldn't even say I hated you.

I mean to say,

I never cared enough

In the first place.

You aren't worth my

'feelings'

I love the sun,

The sand,

The sea.

Can't stand reading,

Writing,

Rain.

You'd never see me in a library,

You can catch me in a party somewhere.

I'll never stop talking,

It's not a thing I can do.

Do you think you know me yet?

You probably do.

But of course,

I've been lying to you the whole time.

You don't know anything about me.

And yet while thinking you knew me,

Your pre-conceived opinion took form.

Based on my lies,

You like me,

Perhaps not?

You might've fallen for my lies,

Maybe you didn't.

Who's to know?

Not me, I don't know you.

And I will never pretend I do.

A graveyard of ghosts.

People I never knew.

Spirits stuck on the wrong side of the light.

If ever you've walked

Through names on headstones,

If ever a breeze has brushed by you,

Consider the hand of the ghost on your shoulder.

It's not there to harm you,

Perhaps it's someone you know.

They have only come to greet you,

Let you know they haven't gone.

So walk through graveyards of ghosts,

Consider the breeze,

The lives of lost spirits

And the love they still carry.

There are a million things I wish to forget.

Embarrassing moments,

Painful memories.

If I could,

I'd physically take them from my head

And throw them in the sea,

Never to be found.

Every time I try to forget,

They are the only things in the forefront of my mind.

I'm not sure I'll ever forget,

Though I wish I could.

Somehow,

Memories over time stop hurting,

But sting that little bit more when remembered.

I spend most of my time

Remembering.

When it's all I want,

To forget.

79

Even the most beautiful of places

Fall victim to the darkness of night.

But even within the black,

The landscape is still wonderful.

So do not be afraid when the darkness in you takes over.

Within,

You are still beautiful as ever.

80

The sky is burning.

Embers are showering everyone and everything.

There is nowhere to run.

We will all burn with the Earth.

The downfall of our own making.

The water is black,

The ground,

Covered in ash.

We've finally realised

What we've done to ourselves.

There's no stopping it now.

The sky is burning.

The heat will engulf us all.

Break her.

Again and again.

But don't be surprised when you're the one who bleeds.

Next time remember,

She is a flower.

But touch her,

You'll find her thorns.

'Man's best friend.'

While I am no man,

You are truly the best friend I've ever known.

The little beastie who always finds the way to my heart.

While you're grown now,

In my eyes,

You'll always be tiny.

I've given you many names,

But Bug will always be my favourite.

I imagine before she left,

Your predecessor taught you some things about me.

The way you stand on me when I cry,

Exactly how to beg for food.

We may not speak the same language,

But I love you,

More than any words,

Foreign or not,

Could express.

83

It feels as though I've been awake for an age.

Every sound has been heightened.

Every sight amplified.

Who knows what's real and what's not?

I seem to have lost track of the seconds passing by,

The ticking of the clock almost inaudible now.

I don't know what the time is.

Goodnight.

Good morning?

Oh I don't know anymore.

Time is an abstract construct,

I will not try to solve the universe right now.

There are times I wish you could read my mind.

There are times I pray you cannot.

You occupy most of my thoughts,

As the main character of all of my stories.

I wish you could see it all,

At the same time I hope you never know.

Do not infiltrate my thoughts

But make them your own.

Take over my mind

As you have done unknowingly.

My brainwaves match yours,

Take as much of me as you want to.

I will not protest.

I was designed and made for

You.

I've been told so many times

To enjoy my youth,

Be a child while I can.

But I don't know that I was ever truly a child.

Perhaps in my early days,

But childhood was lost from before the word teen.

I know responsibility,

I know control.

I do not however know how to relinquish my hold,

And be a child.

To have fun without worry is not a skill I have.

I have been in adult mentality for too long.

I have been mature for my age since my age was a single digit.

Now it is what I look forward to.

To be an adult in age and have my maturity excused.

I want not to be my age.

But I must wait a few years yet.

I must walk through 14,15,16,17

Before I can run at 18.

Waiting for a phone call.

Expecting the worst.

I'm waiting for it to ring.

I'm waiting to answer and hear not your voice but a stranger's.

Counting the minutes,

Envisioning disaster.

I'm waiting to confirm I'm alone again.

I'm wondering if you'll come back to me.

I've made escape routes,

Safety plans,

I know what I'd do if I had to.

Instead you walk through the door.

Safe and unharmed.

I can breathe.

We are okay.

We no longer sing in the halls of this building.

Its rafters do not chill us as we drink.

Friendships gone cold and buried in the ground.

Tables and chairs made barren,

A community gone to waste.

We now do not know these windows and walls,

This place an empty shell of what it once was.

Tomorrow was filled with hope,

Now tomorrow doesn't exist.

I still hear their voices echoed in the stone,

Why am I to return to here,

When the friends I had are gone?

I do not know why it must be this way,

But the phantoms that haunt the windows will watch from here forevermore.

Two people could not be more different.

You are two sides of a very strange world.

Others would say the sight of you walking side by side

Is odd,

But I've found recently that opposites can match.

Completely different may you be,

But you seem to work just as well as any.

The wonders of the world never cease to amaze me,

The two of you being the greatest mystery.

The world may not be designed for pairs such as yours,

But you'll always find a way,

No matter what you run into,

You'll find each other,

Your likeness never quite the same.

89

Her.

Everything about her.

The way her eyes light up when she sees a deer.

The slight stumble as she gets out of a car.

How her confidence shines when talking about her interests.

That girl who plays such a part in my life,

She doesn't know it,

She doesn't see how she is the world to me.

But if I ever loved anything,

My love is for

Her.

90

How can I need you as much as I do,

While knowing you'll never come back to me?

You never told me your name.

I never told you mine.

Yet when I looked at you

I felt the rush of warmth that radiated from you.

You liked my clothes,

We matched quite well.

Your red hair accented by the green of your shirt.

And you looked at me.

You looked and you spoke to me.

And for once in my life I found the words.

I'll probably never see you again,

I can't properly make out the features of your face

Though I'm sure it was beautiful.

Perhaps we'll cross paths one day?

For I have not looked at someone and felt as I did

In a long time.

You caused me to lose my thoughts

And have my mind go clear for a few seconds.

You made me *feel* again.

And I never even knew your name.

92

I have made many mistakes in my days.

But none so great as this.

Your sweet words just felt right.

At the time I was not aware

You spoke with a liar's tongue,

Designed to deceive even the most observant.

I have never been hurt like this.

You were meant to be my world,

I told you so.

But to drag me into this place

And burn that world to the ground

In front of my eyes

Along with every belonging I hold dear,

That is why

I never should have gone there.

I will write for others and the world my entire life.

I will use words to describe feelings of

Love,

Heartbreak,

Disaster,

Achievement.

But for once in my life,

I'd like to put down the pen,

Hand it to someone else,

Read something about me,

Without knowing it's every detail.

Just once,

I'd like to be the poem

And not the poet.

94

If outwardly you are this beautiful,
I can't imagine the beauty your soul holds.

I never enjoyed the dark as a child.

It was frightening,

Not knowing what could wait in the dark.

A light resided by my bed at all times,

I would never sleep staring into nothing.

Fast forward to now,

No longer so small and afraid,

The dark is more welcoming,

Friendly.

Everything is soft in the dark.

No harsh lights and lines.

There could be something waiting there,

But I think perhaps

It does not intend to hurt me,

It is just as scared as I was.

96

The snap of the leaf from the branch.

The sudden separation unknown to both.

The tree is without its creation,

The leaf without its maker.

So when I say I miss you,

Think of how the leaf misses its home,

Its safe place,

Think of how it wilts alone,

Think of it,

Then think of me.

97

Our hands touched

And a million things were said

In the blink of an eye.

There are only fleeting moments in which I am happy.

It is not a word I tend to use often.

For how can true happiness be mine

When I live in a world not designed to provide it?

I cannot believe in true happiness

While I know all that I love

Will leave me.

However,

I like my fleeting moments.

They are the tiny good things I find

In an ordinary life,

Where I am just a person,

Not destined for greatness.

I am simply someone who finds joy

In fleeting moments of happiness.

99

'You can't have rainbows without the rain'

Yet the rain is what I wish for.

The colours dazzling the clouds is a sight to see

But the rain is welcoming,

Familiar.

The rain is my favourite,

Purely because it shows,

The sky is crying with us.

Glass shards from the window

The floor glitters from the refracted light.

The iridescence,

Too pretty not too touch,

The red of the rainbows in the light made from the red under my skin.

There is pain in the beauty of objects,

There is pain in the beauty of love,

You want to look at the light,

First you must deal with the glass.

The impossible desire of pretty things,

Too painful to even touch.

You can stare at colours born from glass,

Your hands numb

After the shards held in your hand dug their sharp edges too deep.

You will never learn.

You will keep picking up the glass

Convinced it won't hurt you again.

But it will.

Every time you go back to it.

The glass will cut you

And break you

Again

And again.

Phthalo

Sage

Mint

Viridian

Gorgeous, gorgeous green.

Envy

Persuasion

Serenity

Velvet draped over a dust ridden armchair.

Nature obtains such a range of this colour

And it calls to the wild and the untamed

The connection through the Earth to the soul

From mint ice cream,

The lightest of greens,

To Phthalo,

A favourite of mine,

The darkness inhabits this,

As well as Viridian,

The comfort in the dark and cool of green tinges.

Nature's favourite colour

Tenebris Viridi

The hero falters.

For once he does not know how to save them.

He looks around at the destruction,

The chaos.

And he wonders,

How did it go so wrong?

A shiver through soldiers

The passed and a final goodbye.

He wasn't supposed to be defeated.

Wasn't supposed to abandon the chase,

But here we are,

In the aftermath.

Too little time to spare,

And too many fallen to count.

Lying on the cold concrete I can feel the water filling the dents in the ground.

I've always wanted to do this,

I thought perhaps the rain would disguise the overwhelming pain I am only now feeling.

For the first few minutes it was torture,

The already settled rain invading everything I touched,

The cold of the ground,

The rain in my eyes.

I'm used to it now,

I closed my eyes,

Stopped fighting with myself.

I never want to leave here,

It feels safe now.

There's no one near me.

It's quiet.

I could almost hear whispers in the wind,

The rain a comforting sensation.

But the rain will stop soon.

I cannot lie here forever.

So goodbye, for now.

Acknowledgements

For the creation of this book, my first thank you goes to my family, who encourage me to be the best I can be, celebrate my achievements and who help to pick me up when I need it. To my teachers, my writing has greatly improved under your guidance, for that I thank you, for reading my work and celebrating it with me and for generally just putting up with me.

In particular, to Miss Fox, Mrs Barnes, and Miss Cochran, who have all been some of my biggest supporters in my writing journey, thank you.

Lastly, I want to acknowledge myself for the work and time I put into this book, it was a challenge but very fun to do. I knew it was going to take a while, which was a daunting thought knowing my impatience, but I continued to remind myself throughout the writing that it would be worth it in the end.

This book is very much representative of me, in many ways. I hope you enjoyed this little look into my life.

About the author

Ruby Moon Churchill is an Autistic, 14-year-old Author and poet from Somerset, England. They enjoy reading and writing as well as creative activities and archery. They began writing in early 2020 and use it as an outlet for things they find hard to say. As their writing became more of a regular thing, they began focusing on works about mental health, love and being a young, queer person in today's society. 'If I Were Fiction' is Ruby's first book, designed to evoke a variety of emotions, recall people, experiences and places that mean something to you, while being enjoyable to read.

Printed in Great Britain
by Amazon